Felix Pastorius

Hot Dog Dinners for 4 String Electric Bass

All rights reserved. No part of this publication may be reproduced, distributed, or transmitted in any form or by any means, including photocopying, recording, or other electronic or mechanical methods, without the prior written permission of the author, Felix Pastorius.

Major Diatonic Modes — 5
Arpeggios Starting on the Root — 7
Arpeggios Starting on the 3rd — 14
Arpeggios Starting on the 5th — 21
Variation #1 — 28
Voice Leading 7th Chords — 29

Harmonic Minor Modes — 30
Arpeggios Starting on the Root — 32
Arpeggios Starting on the 3rd — 39
Arpeggios Starting on the 5th — 46
Variation #2 — 53
Voice Leading 7th Chords — 54

Harmonic Major Modes — 55
Arpeggios Starting on the Root — 57
Arpeggios Starting on the 3rd — 64
Arpeggios Starting on the 5th — 71
Variation #3 — 78
Voice Leading 7th Chords — 79

Melodic Minor Modes — 80
Arpeggios Starting on the Root — 82
Arpeggios Starting on the 3rd — 89
Arpeggios Starting on the 5th — 96
Variation #4 — 103
Voice Leading 7th Chords — 104

1. I wrote this book as a vehicle for exploration.
2. Technique is derived from tone and not injuring yourself.
3. Practicing slow and correct is always more productive than practicing fast and incorrect.
4. At least 50% of the time the most important note is the one you don't play.
5. Music is empathy.

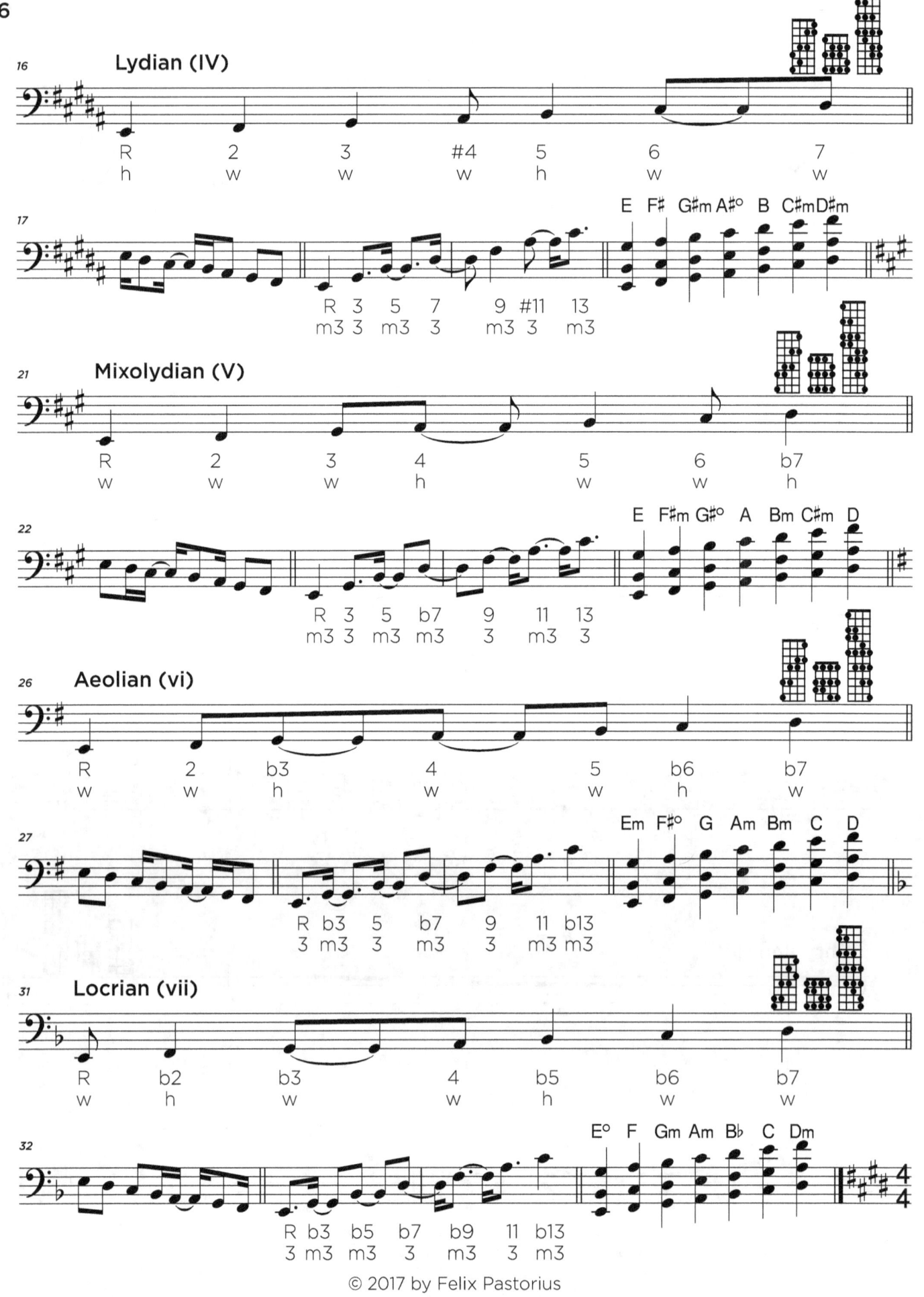

Arpeggios Starting on the Root

© 2017 by Felix Pastorius

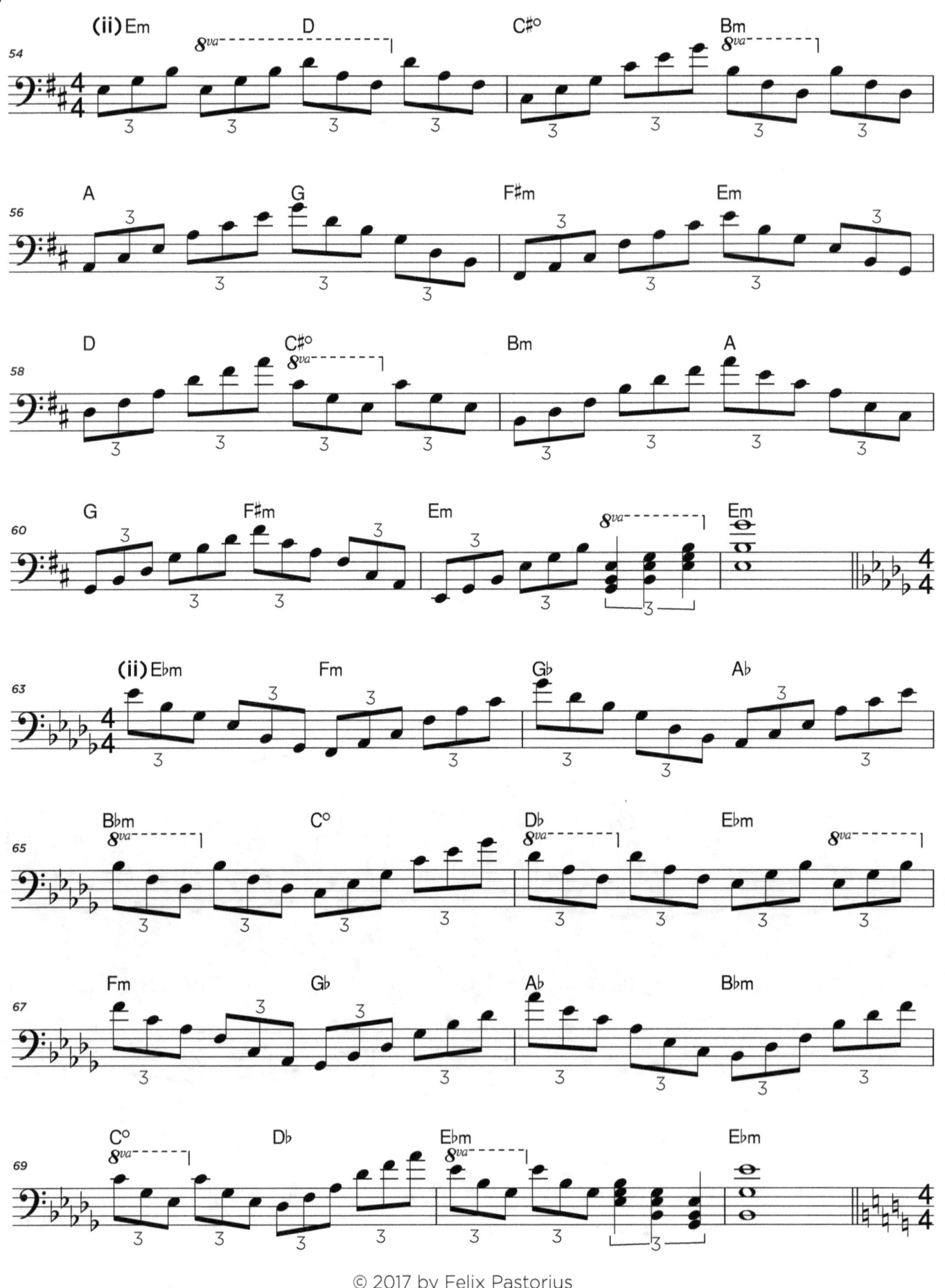

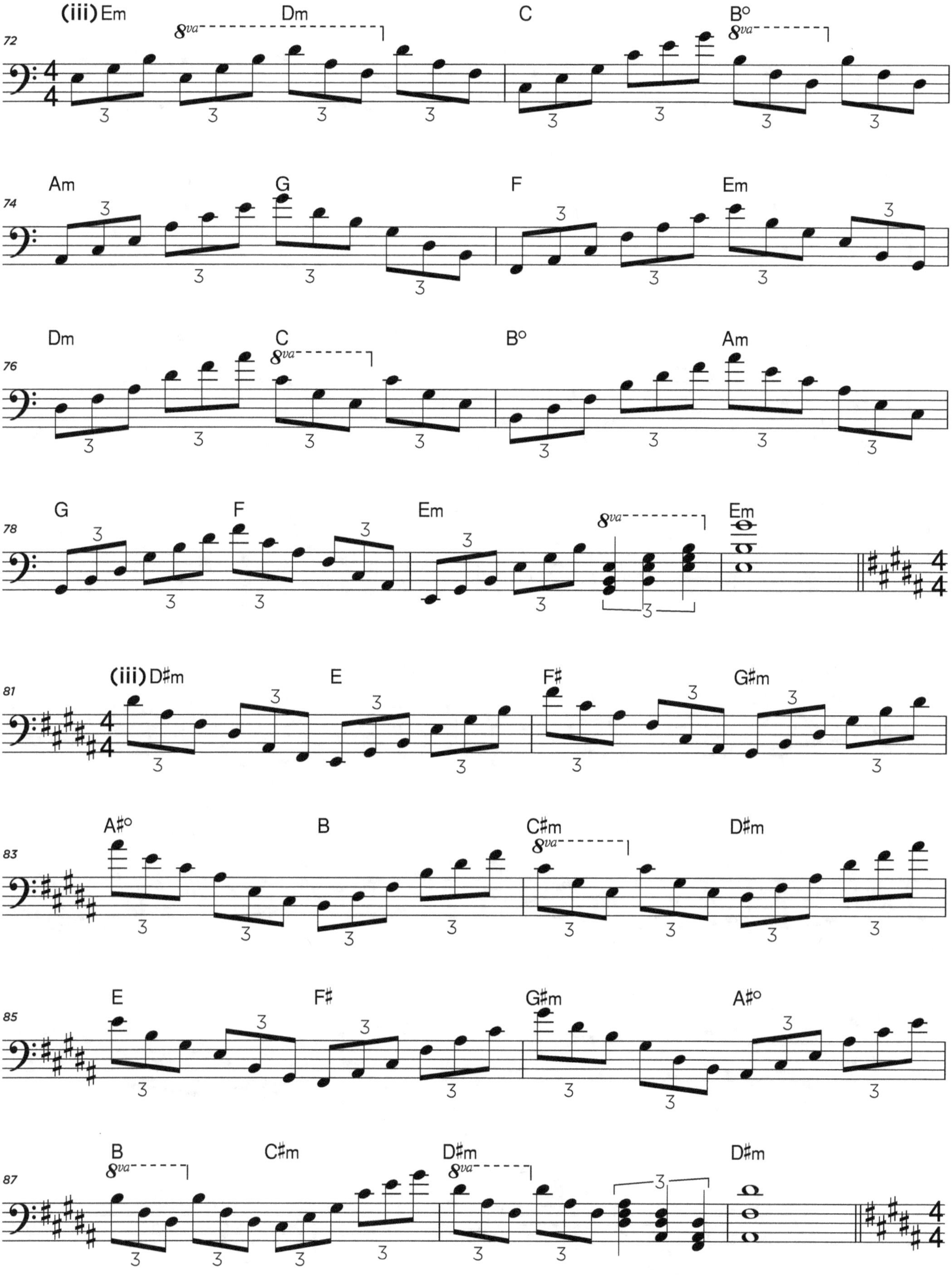
(iii) Em
Dm
C
B°
8va
72
Am
G
F
Em
74
Dm
C
B°
Am
76
G
F
Em
Em
78
(iii) D♯m
E
F♯
G♯m
81
A♯°
B
C♯m
D♯m
83
E
F♯
G♯m
A♯°
85
B
C♯m
D♯m
D♯m
87

© 2017 by Felix Pastorius

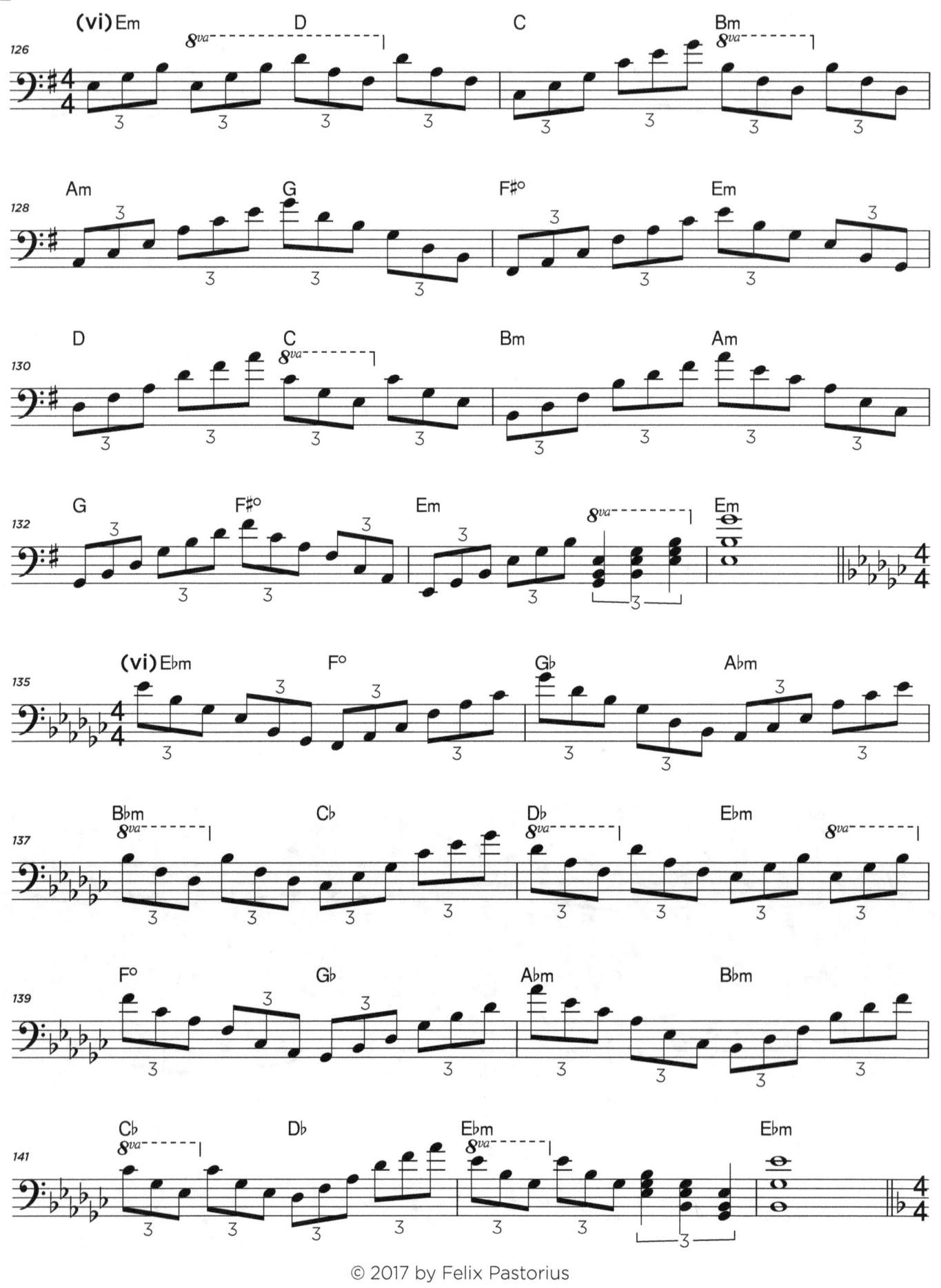

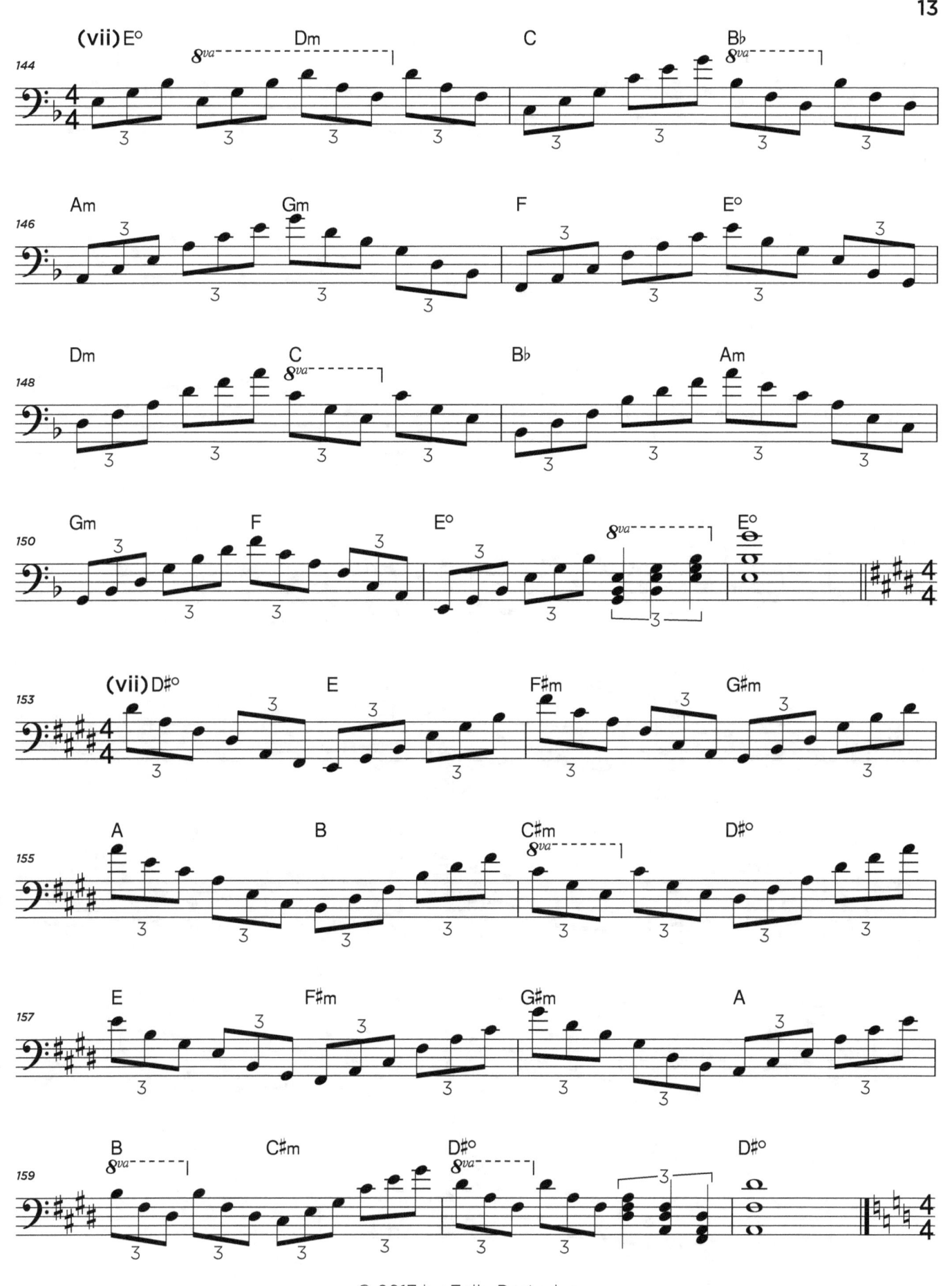

Arpeggios Starting on the 3rd

© 2017 by Felix Pastorius

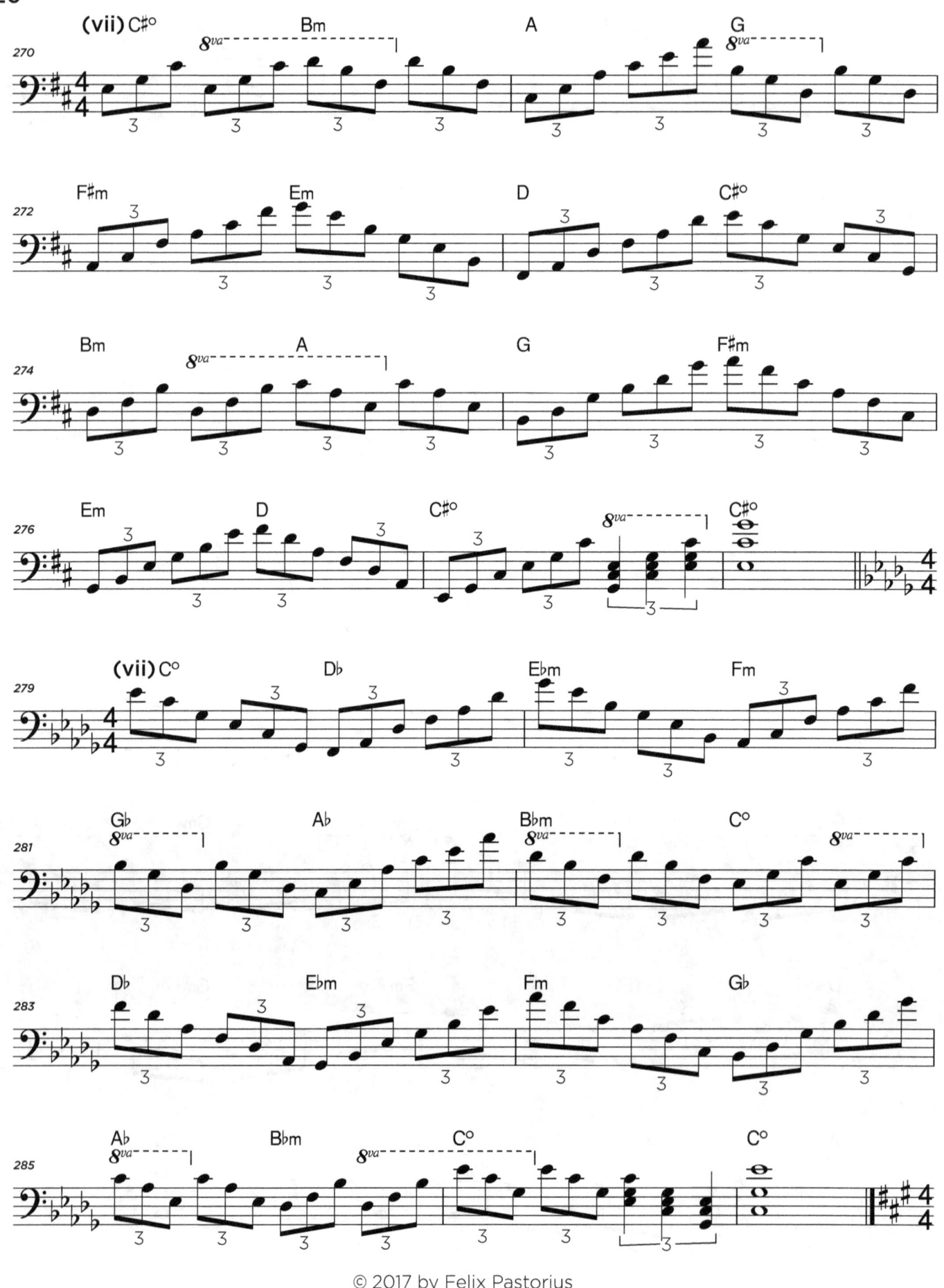

Arpeggios Starting on the 5th

© 2017 by Felix Pastorius

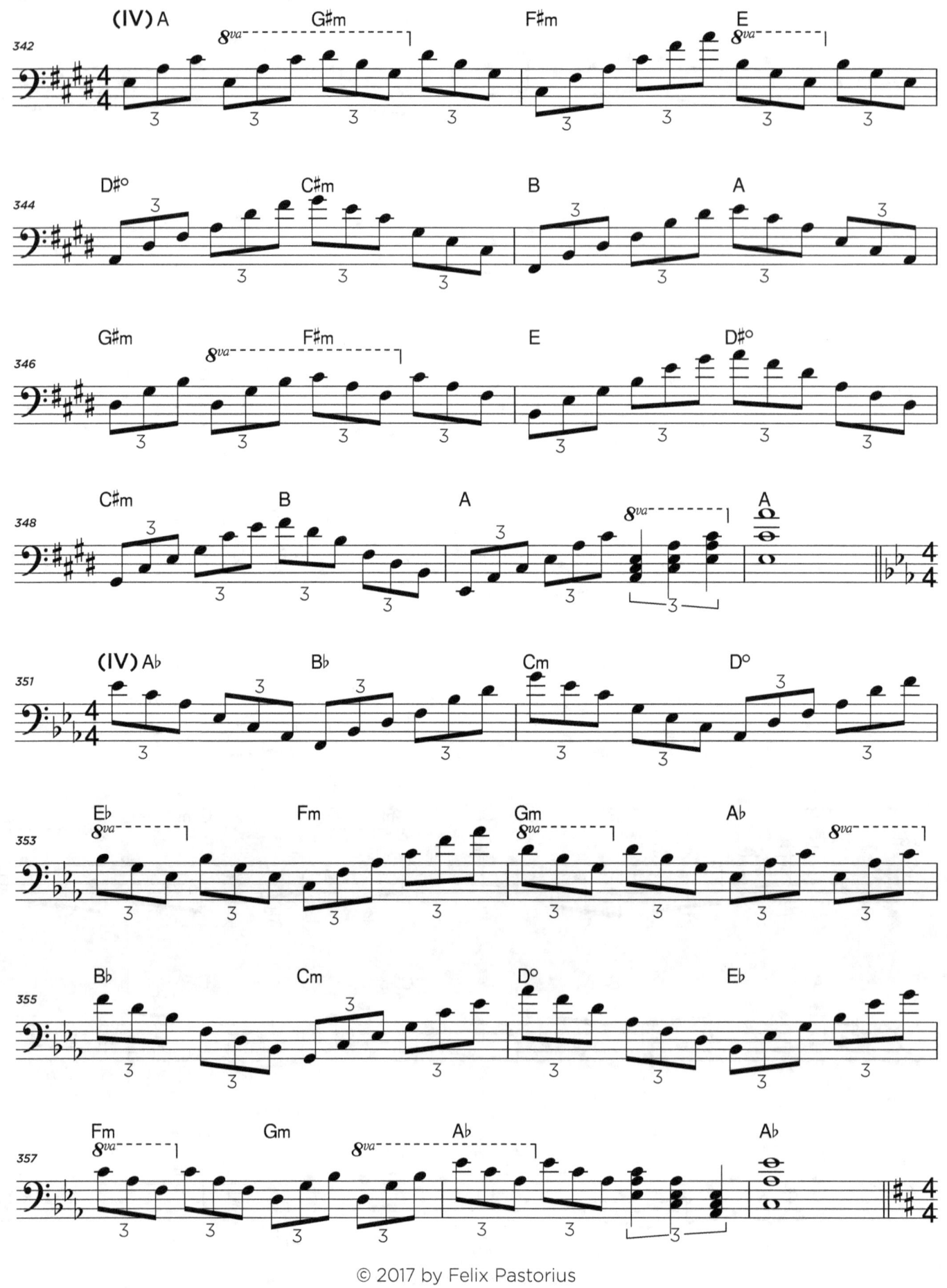

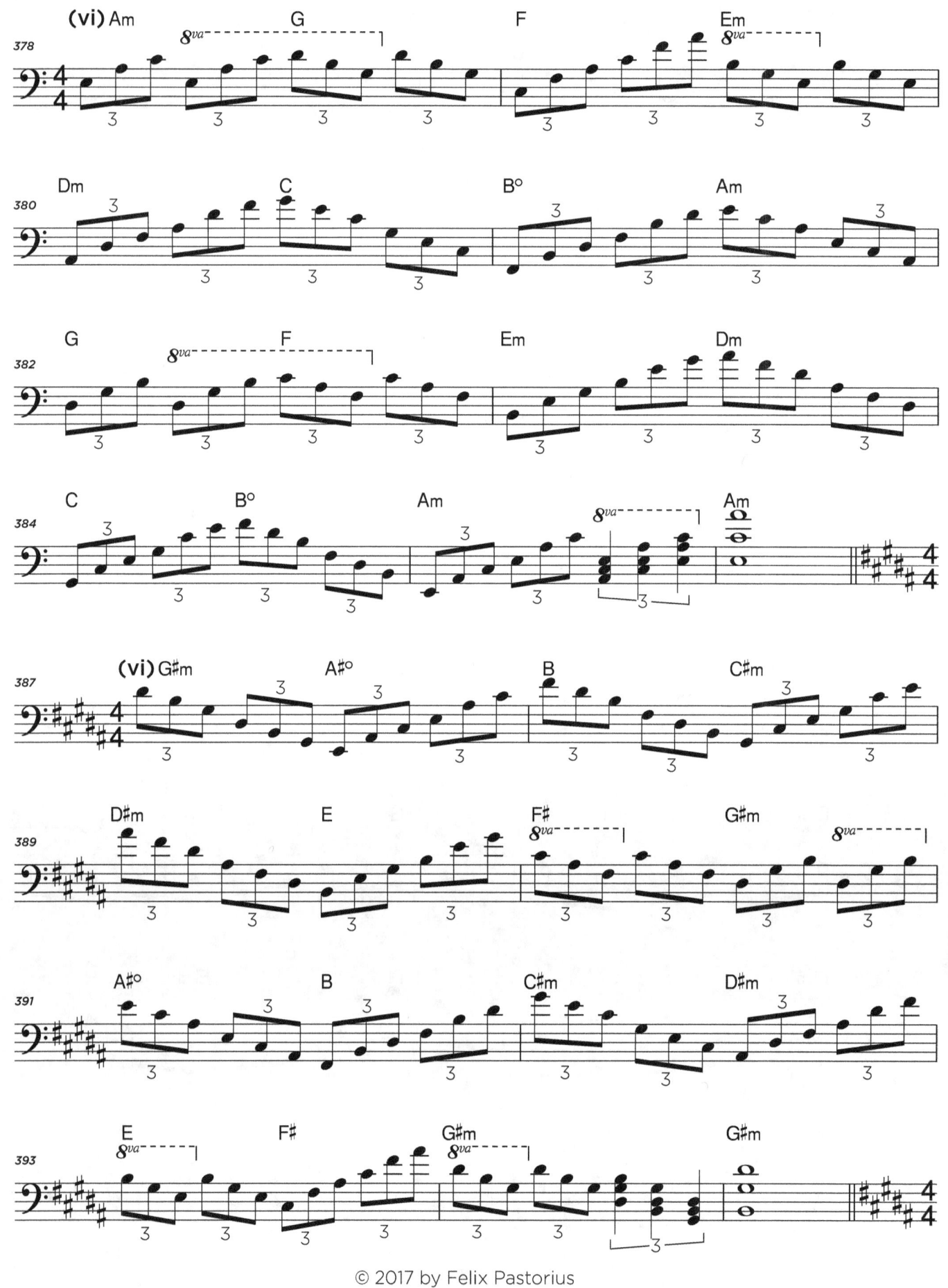

Variation #1

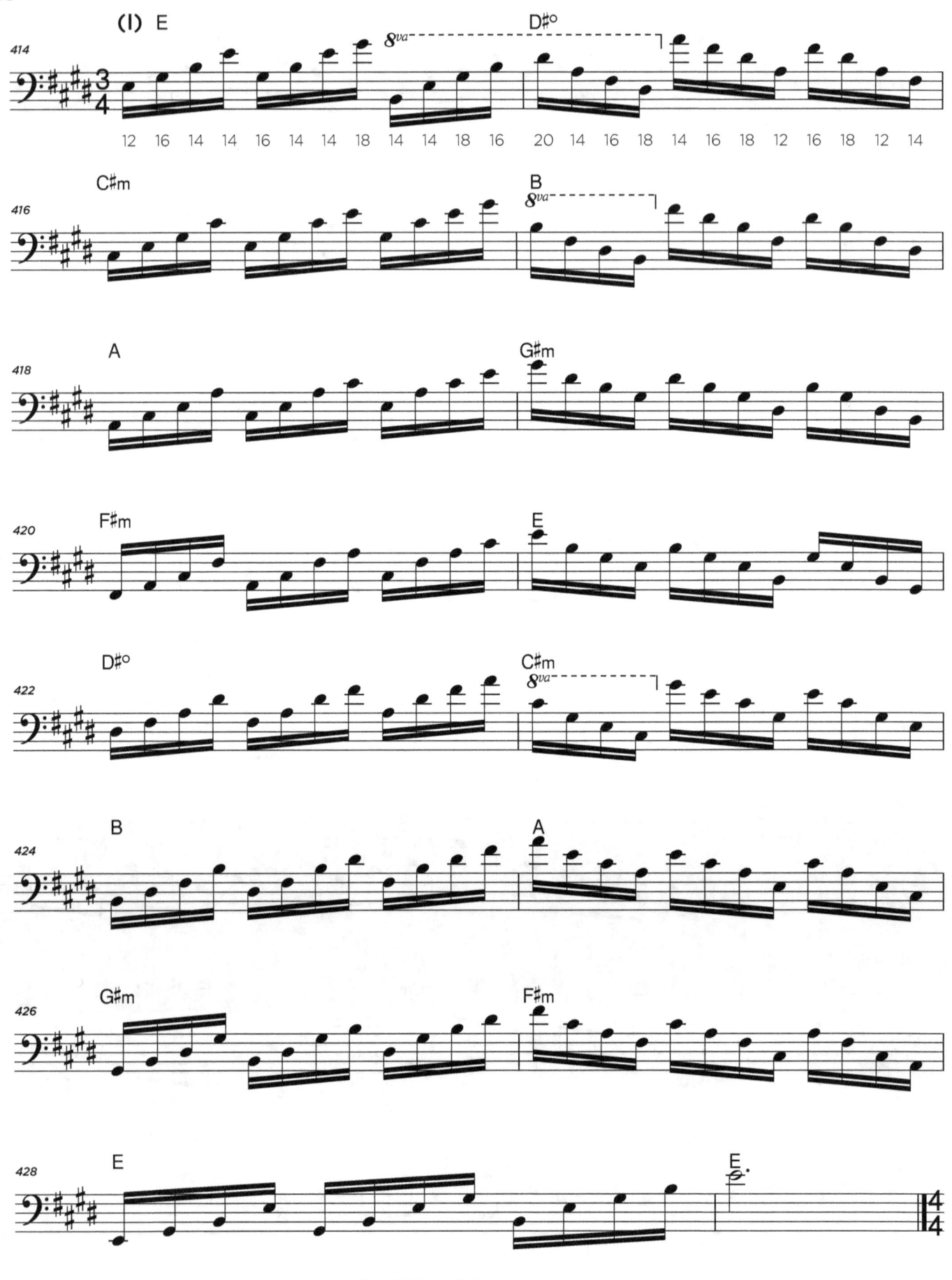

Voice Leading 7th Chords

Harmonic Minor Modes

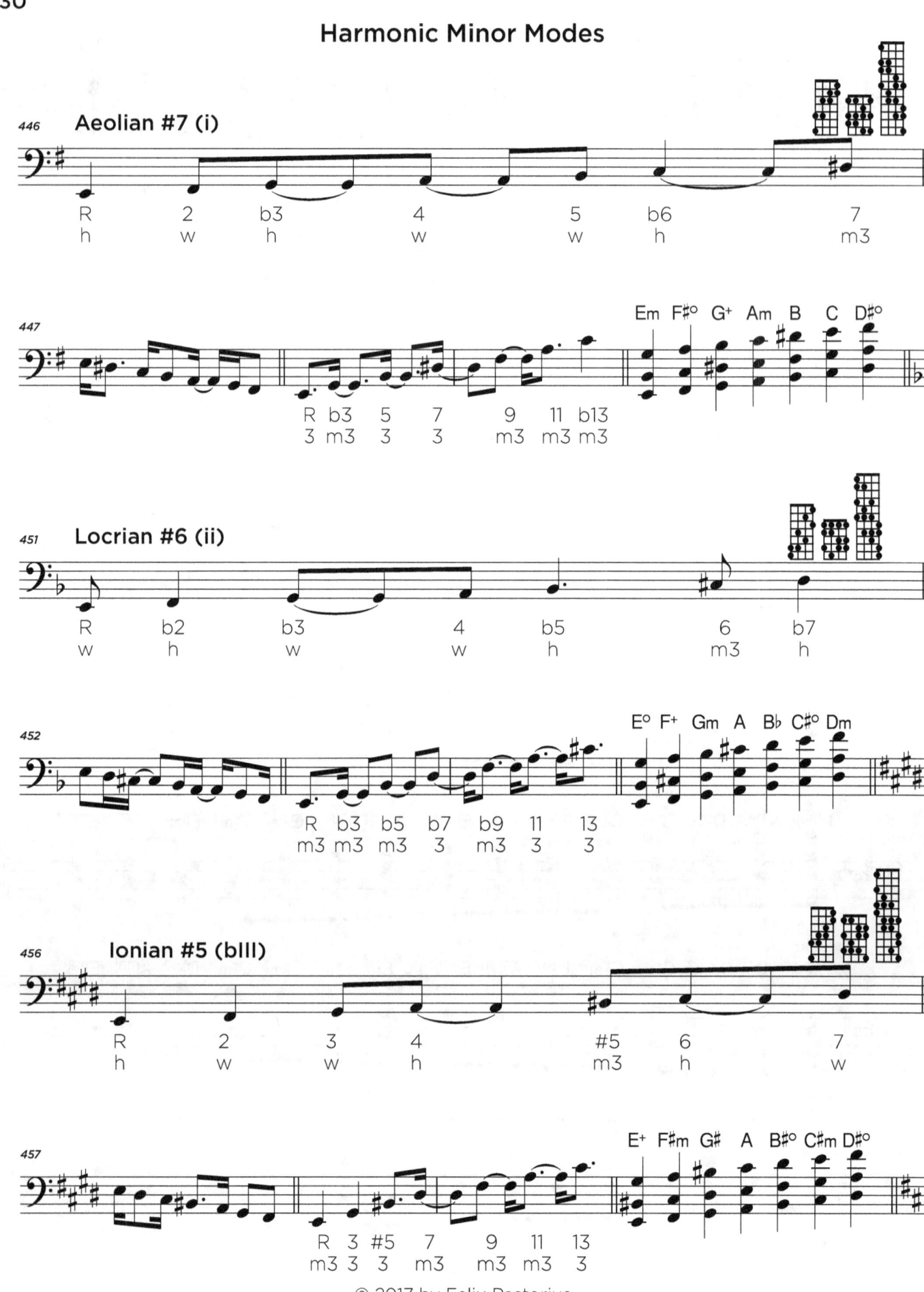

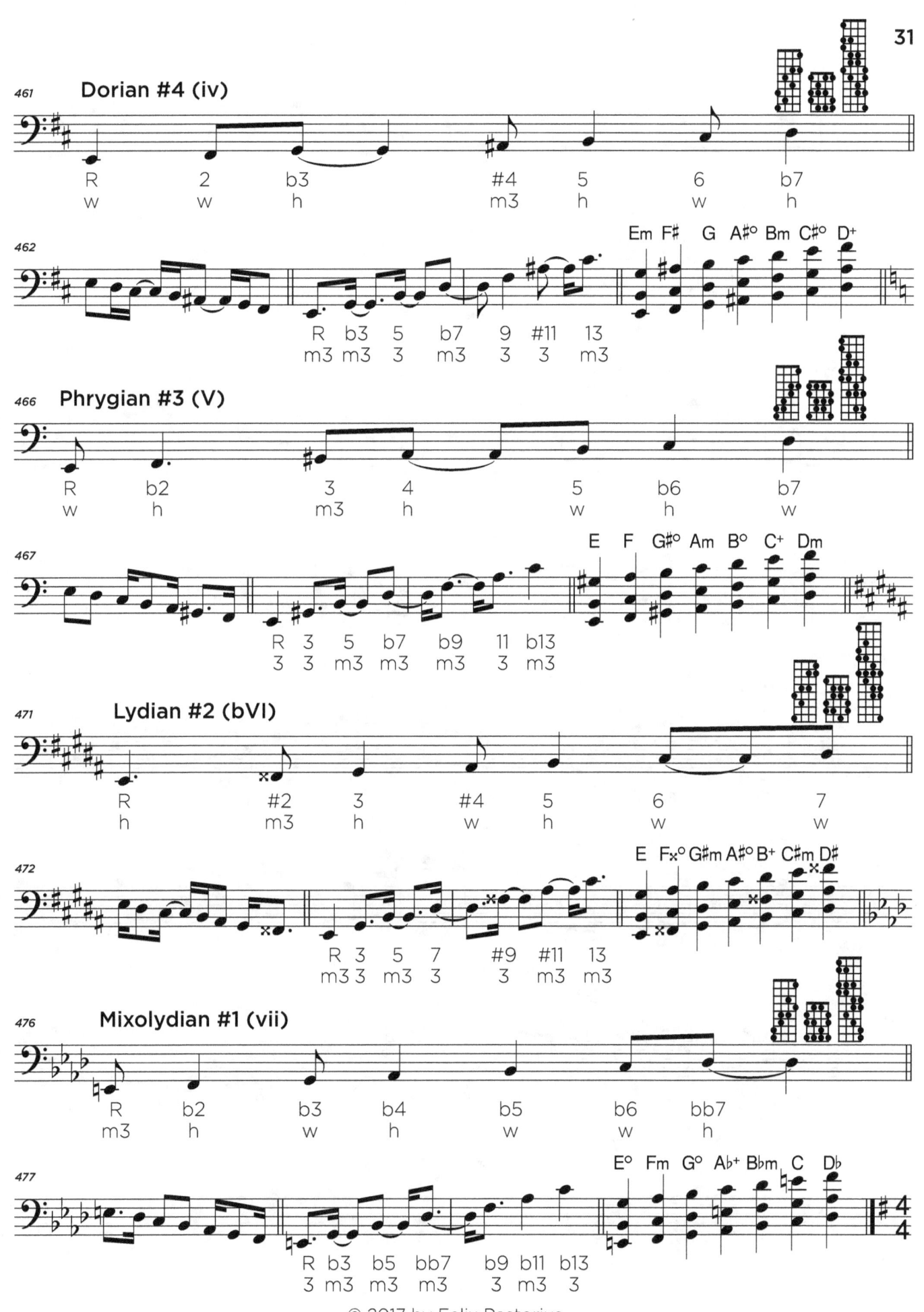

Arpeggios Starting on the Root

© 2017 by Felix Pastorius

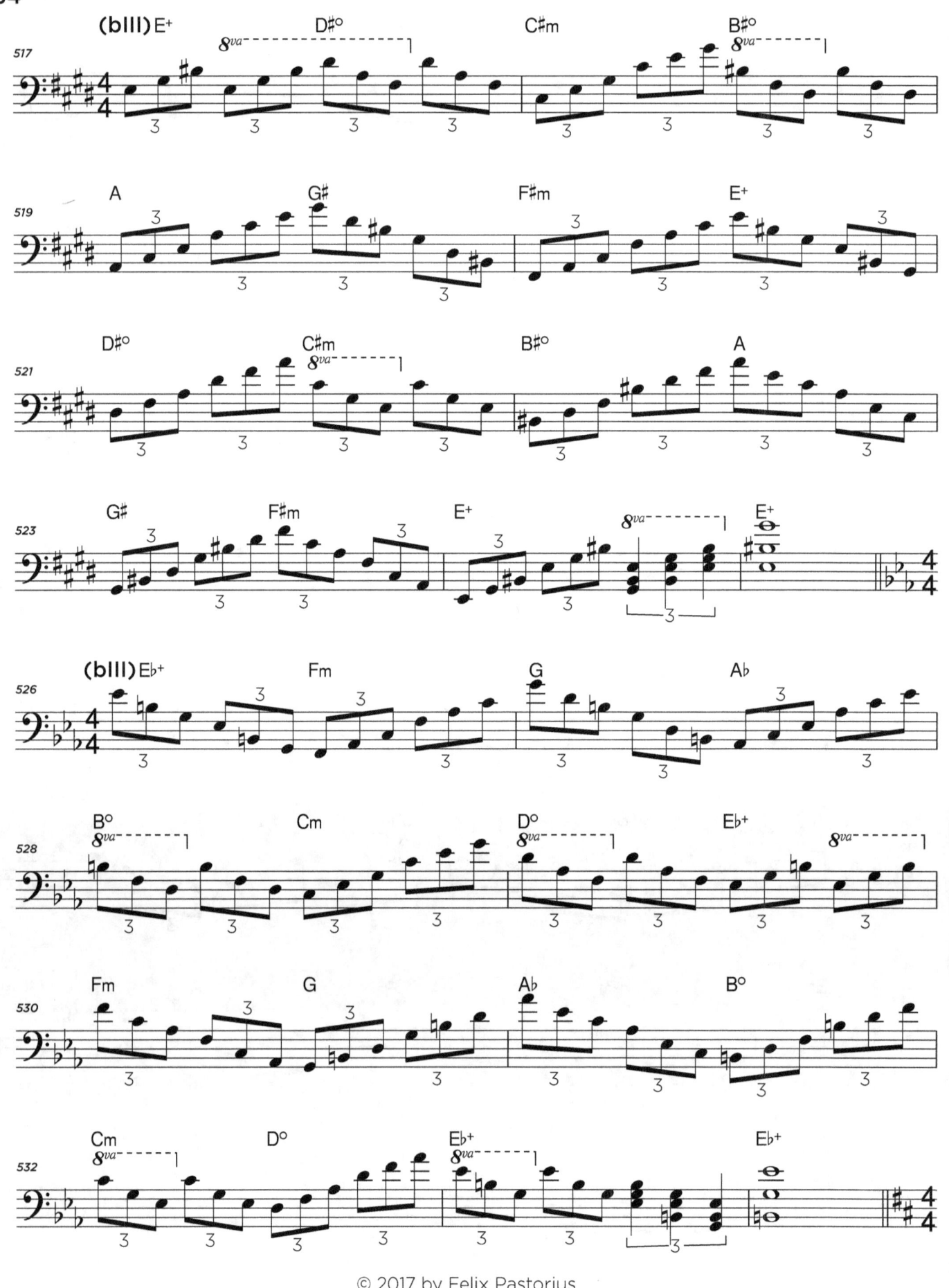

Arpeggios Starting on the 3rd

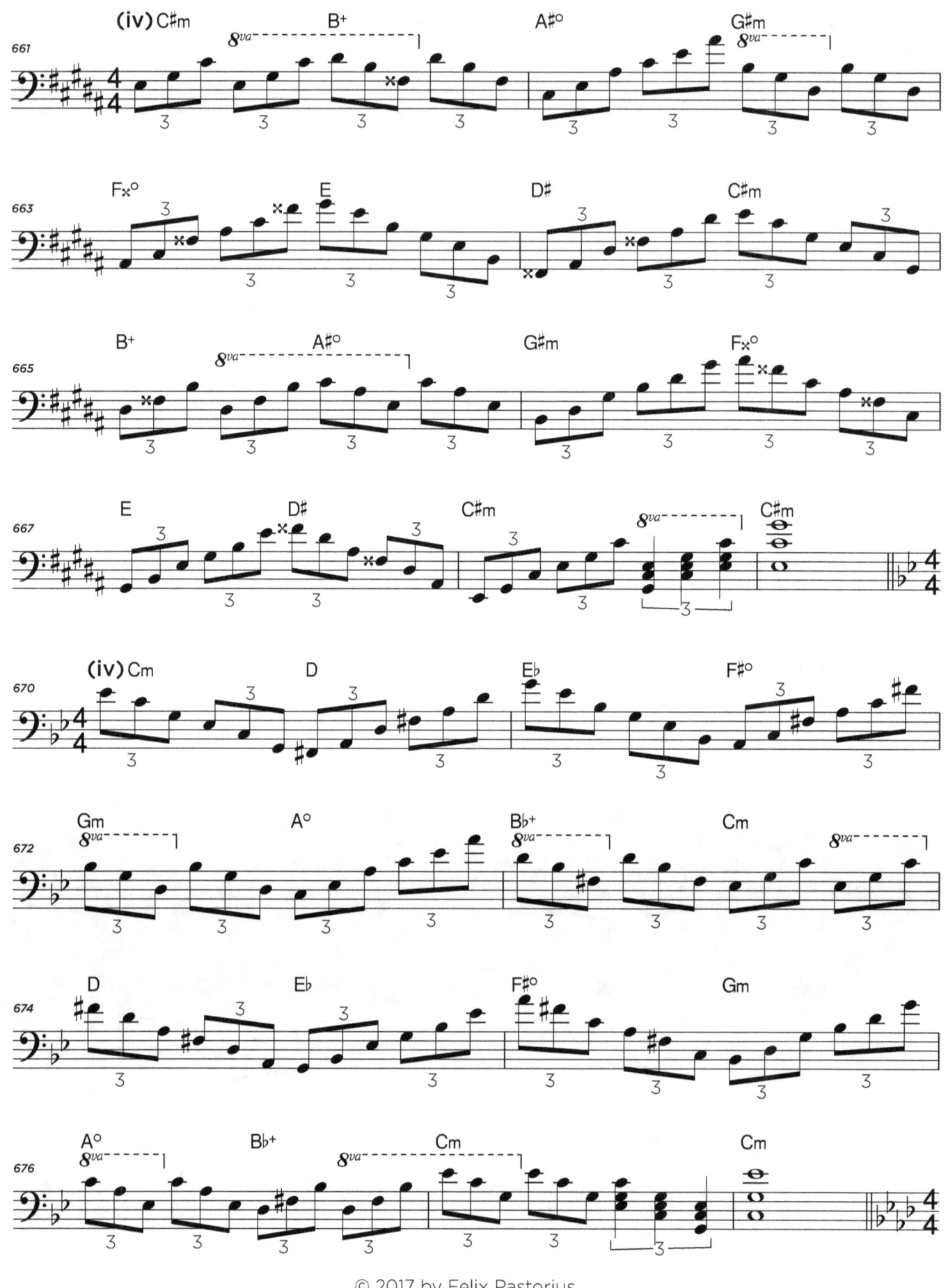

Arpeggios Starting on the 5th

Variation #2

Voice Leading 7th Chords

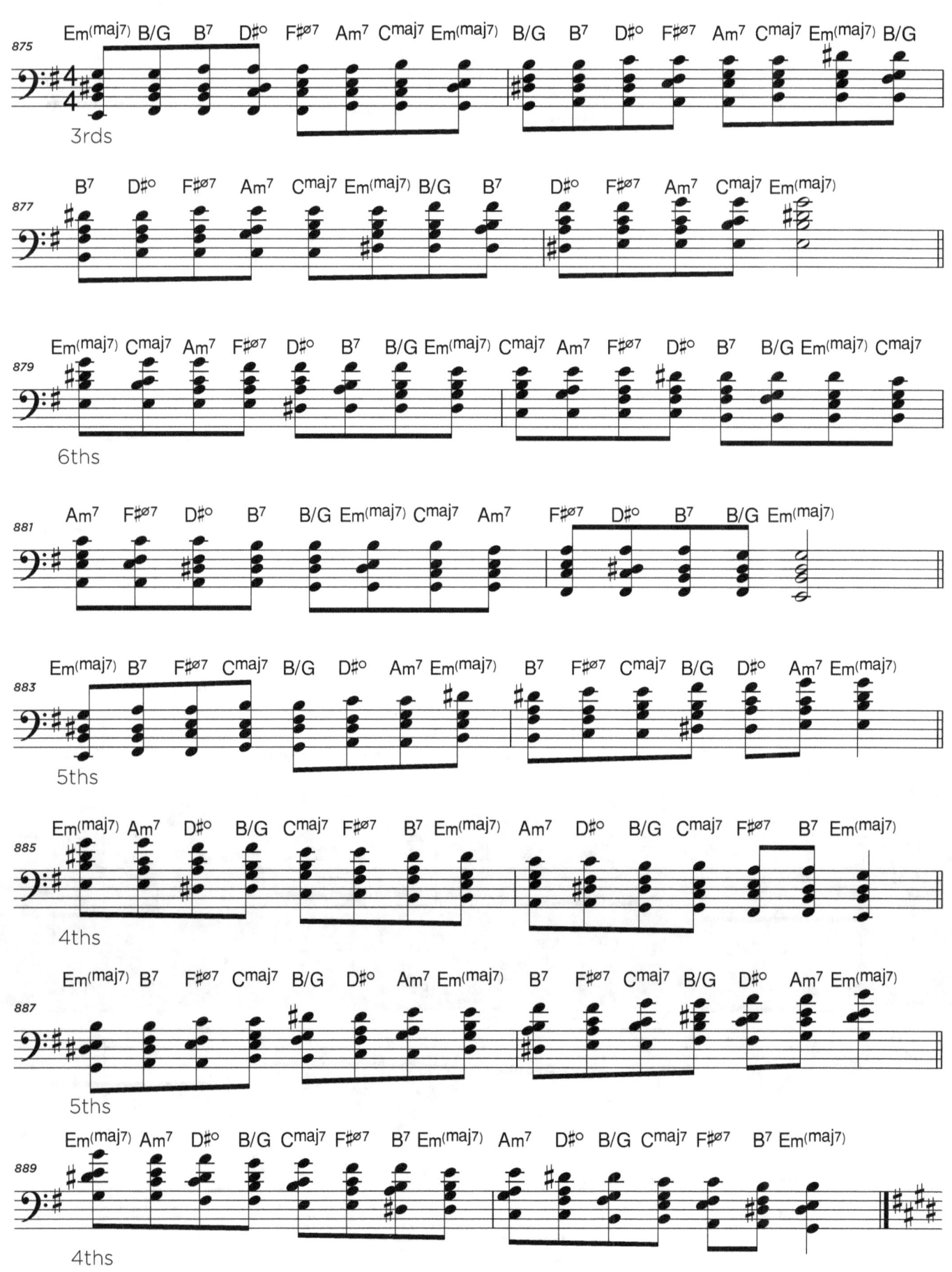

Harmonic Major Modes

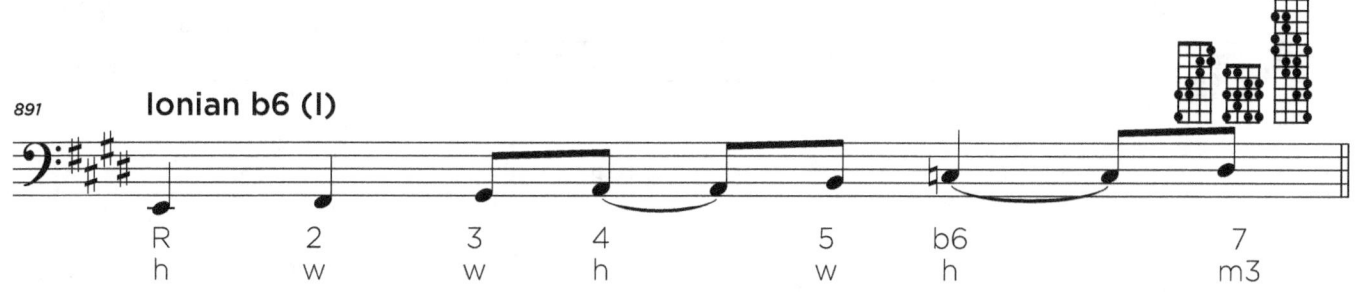

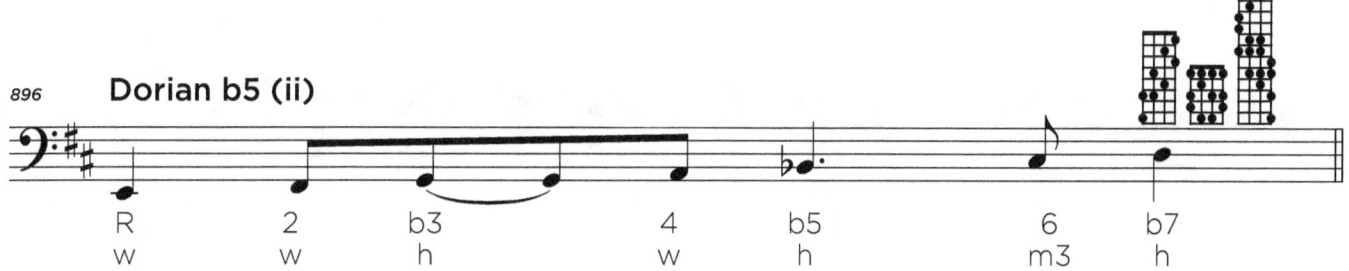

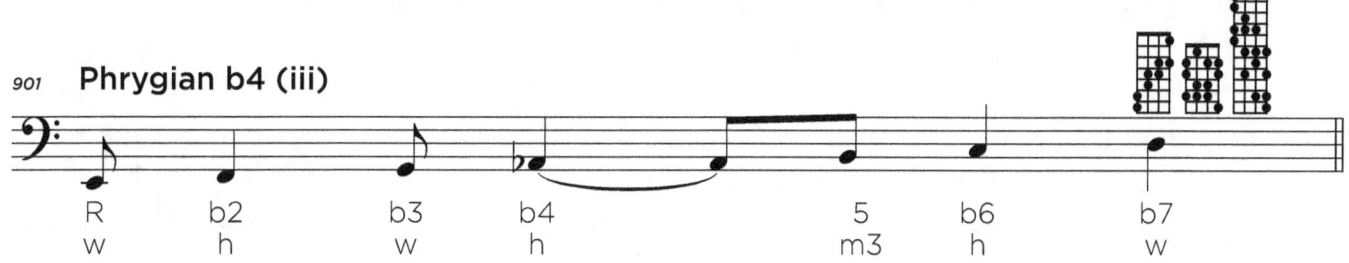

© 2017 by Felix Pastorius

Lydian b3 (iv)

906

R	2	b3	#4	5	6	7
h	w	h	m3	h	w	w

907

Em F# G+ A#° B C#° D#m

R	b3	5	7	9	#11	13
m3	m3	3	3	m3	3	m3

Mixolydian b2 (V)

911

R	b2	3	4	5	6	b7
w	h	m3	h	w	w	h

912

E F+ G#° A B° C#m Dm

R	3	5	b7	b9	11	13
m3	3	m3	m3	m3	3	3

Aeolian b1 (bVI)

916

R	#2	3	#4	#5	6	7
h	m3	h	w	w	h	w

917

Fb+ G° Ab Bb° Cm Dbm Eb

R	3	#5	7	#9	#11	13
m3	3	3	m3	3	m3	m3

Locrian b7 (vii)

921

R	b2	b3	4	b5	b6	bb7
m3	h	w	w	h	w	h

922

E° F G° Am Bbm C Db+

R	b3	b5	bb7	b9	11	b13
3	m3	m3	m3	3	3	m3

© 2017 by Felix Pastorius

Arpeggios Starting on the Root

Arpeggios Starting on the 3rd

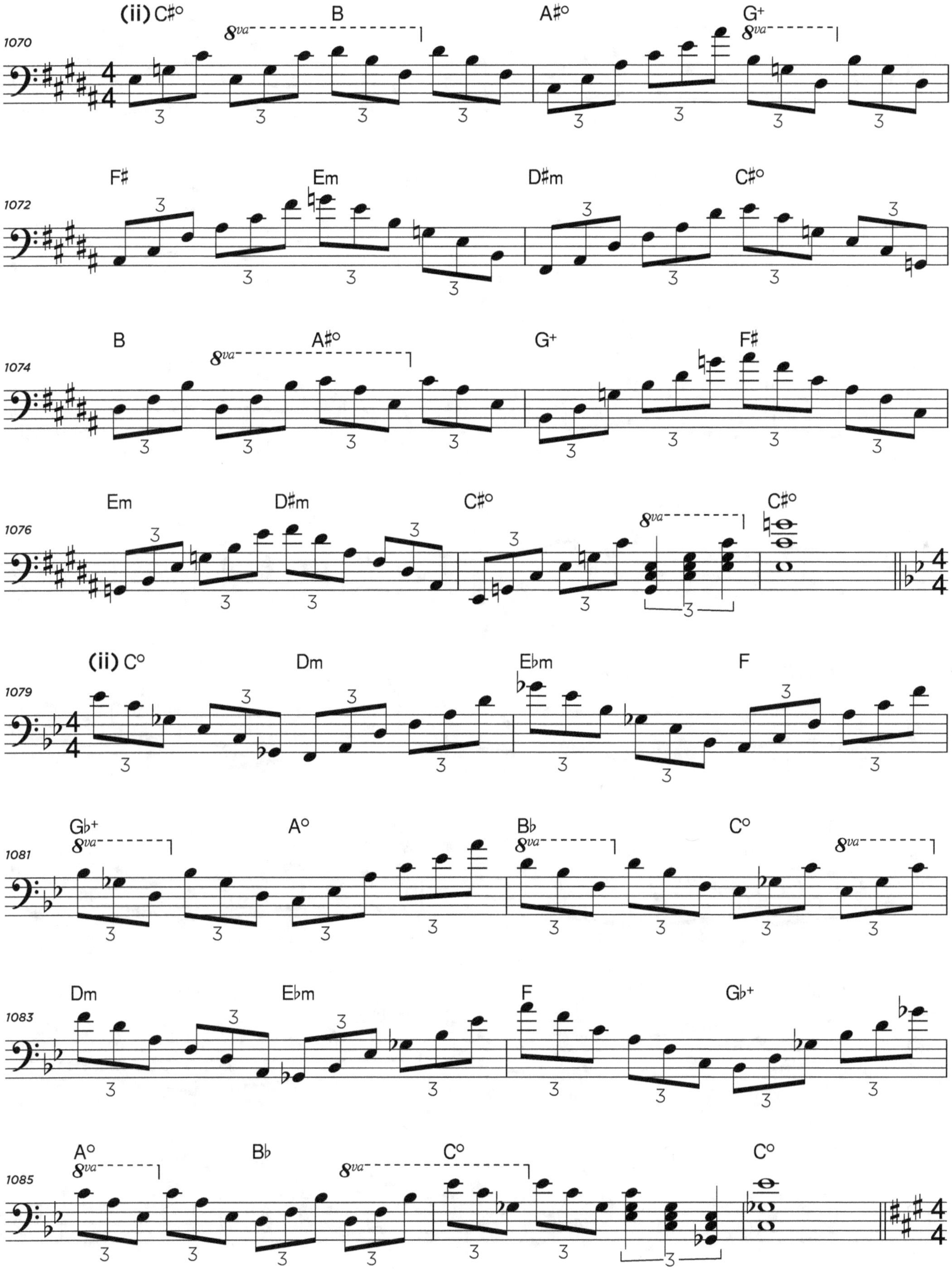
(ii) C♯° B A♯° G+
1070
8va
F♯ Em D♯m C♯°
1072
B A♯° G+ F♯
1074
8va
Em D♯m C♯° C♯°
1076
8va
(ii) C° Dm E♭m F
1079
G♭+ A° B♭ C°
1081
8va
Dm E♭m F G♭+
1083
A° B♭ C° C°
1085
8va

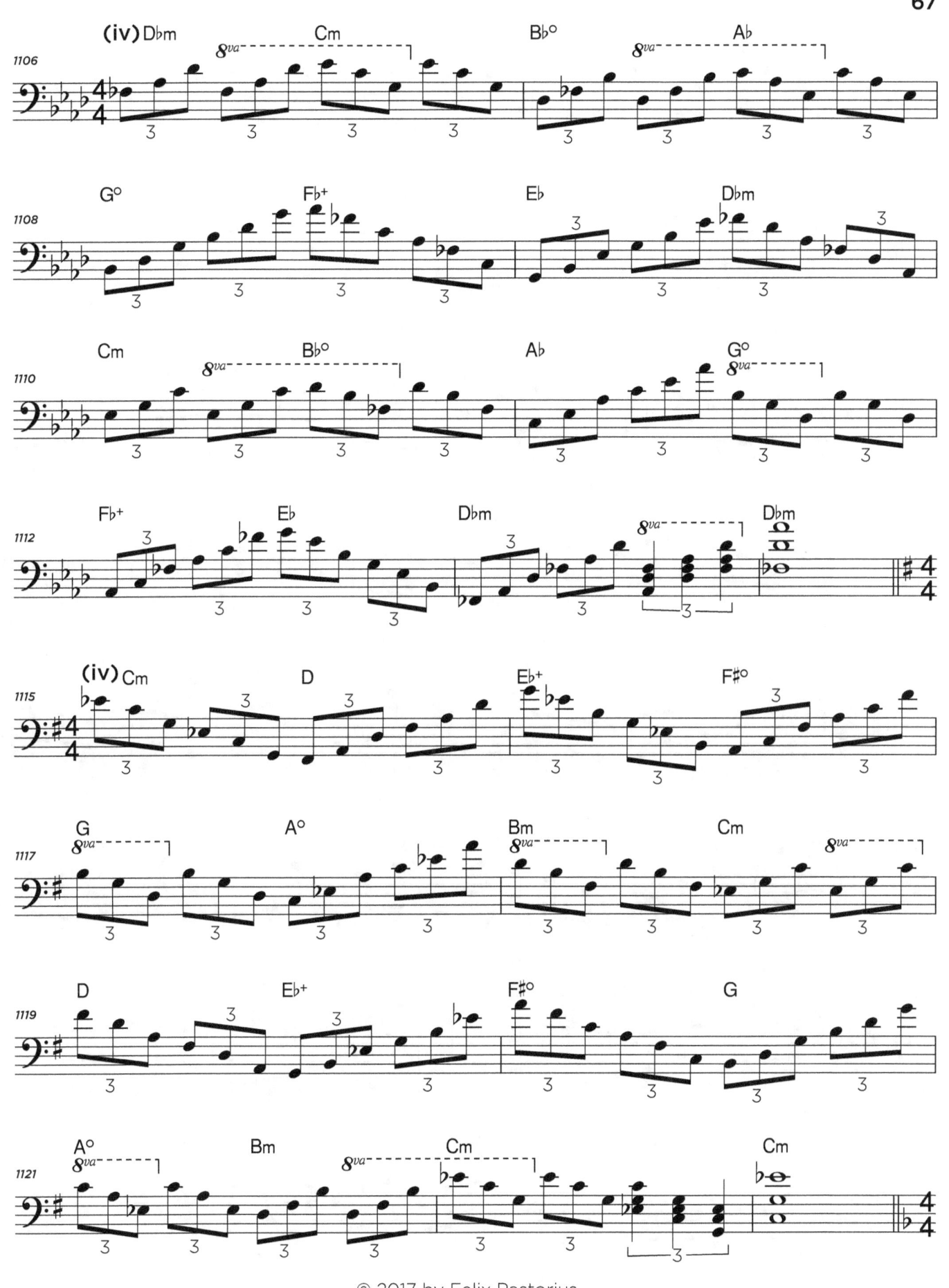

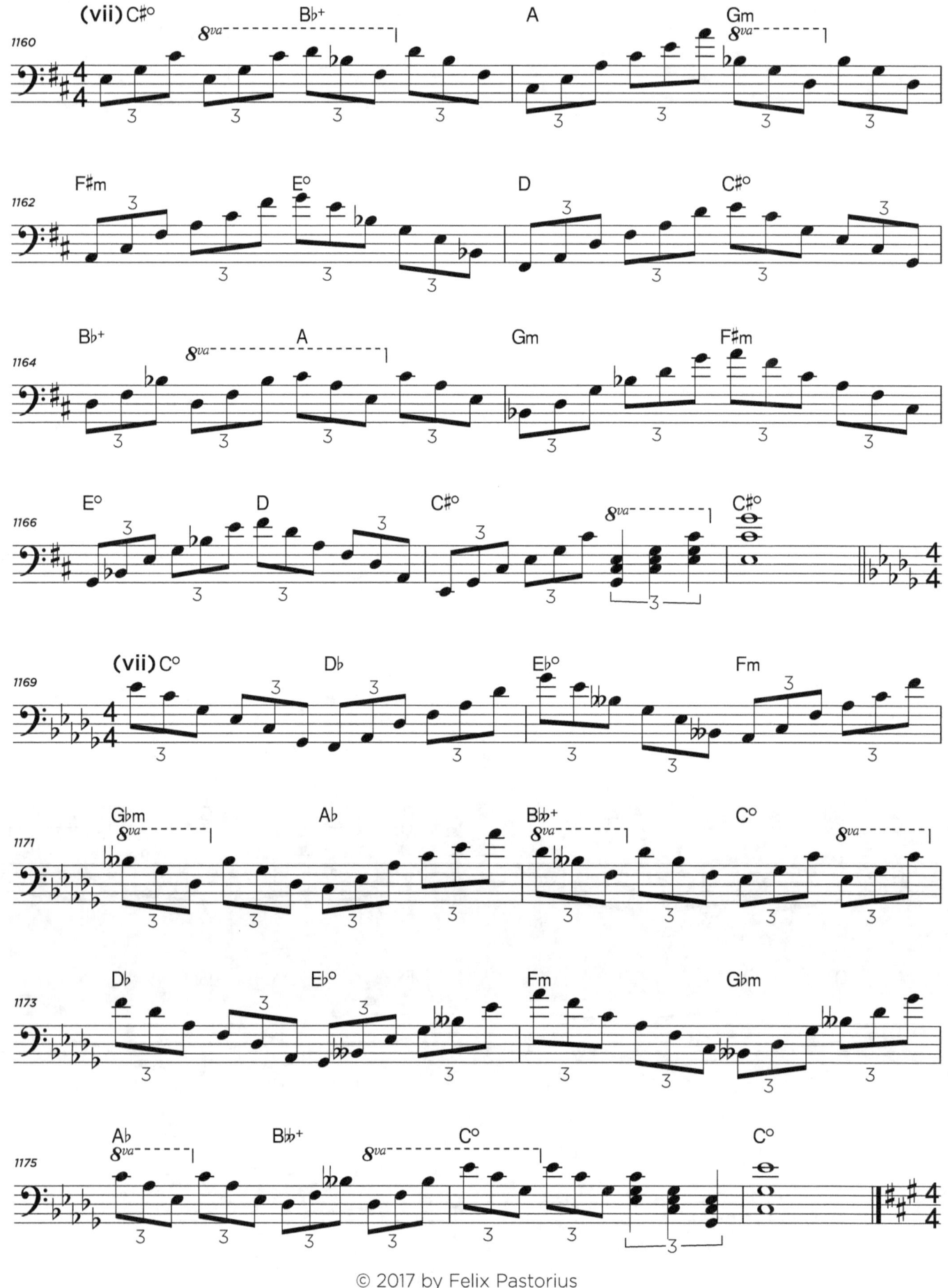

Arpeggios Starting on the 5th

© 2017 by Felix Pastorius

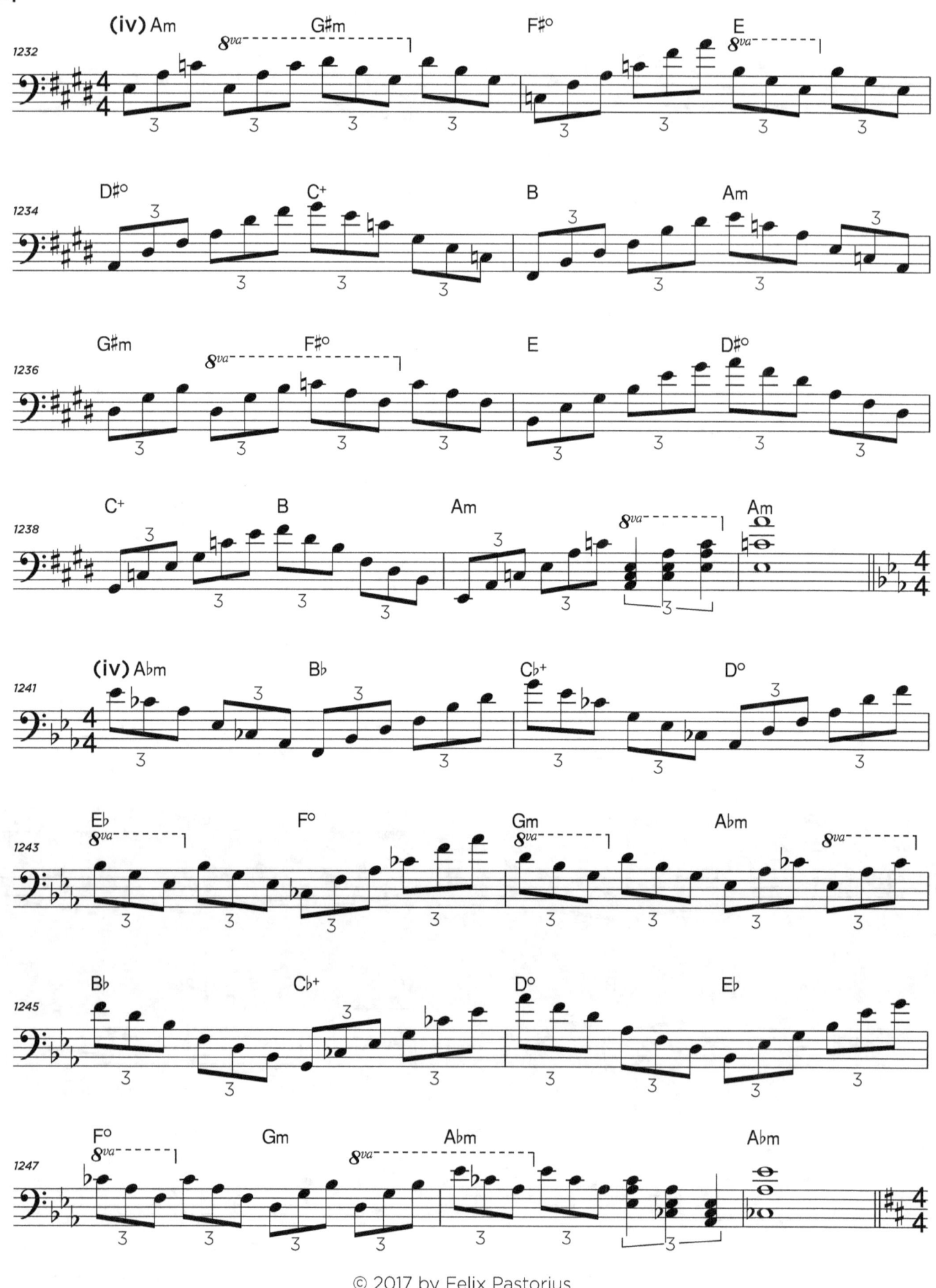

Variation #3

Voice Leading 7th Chords

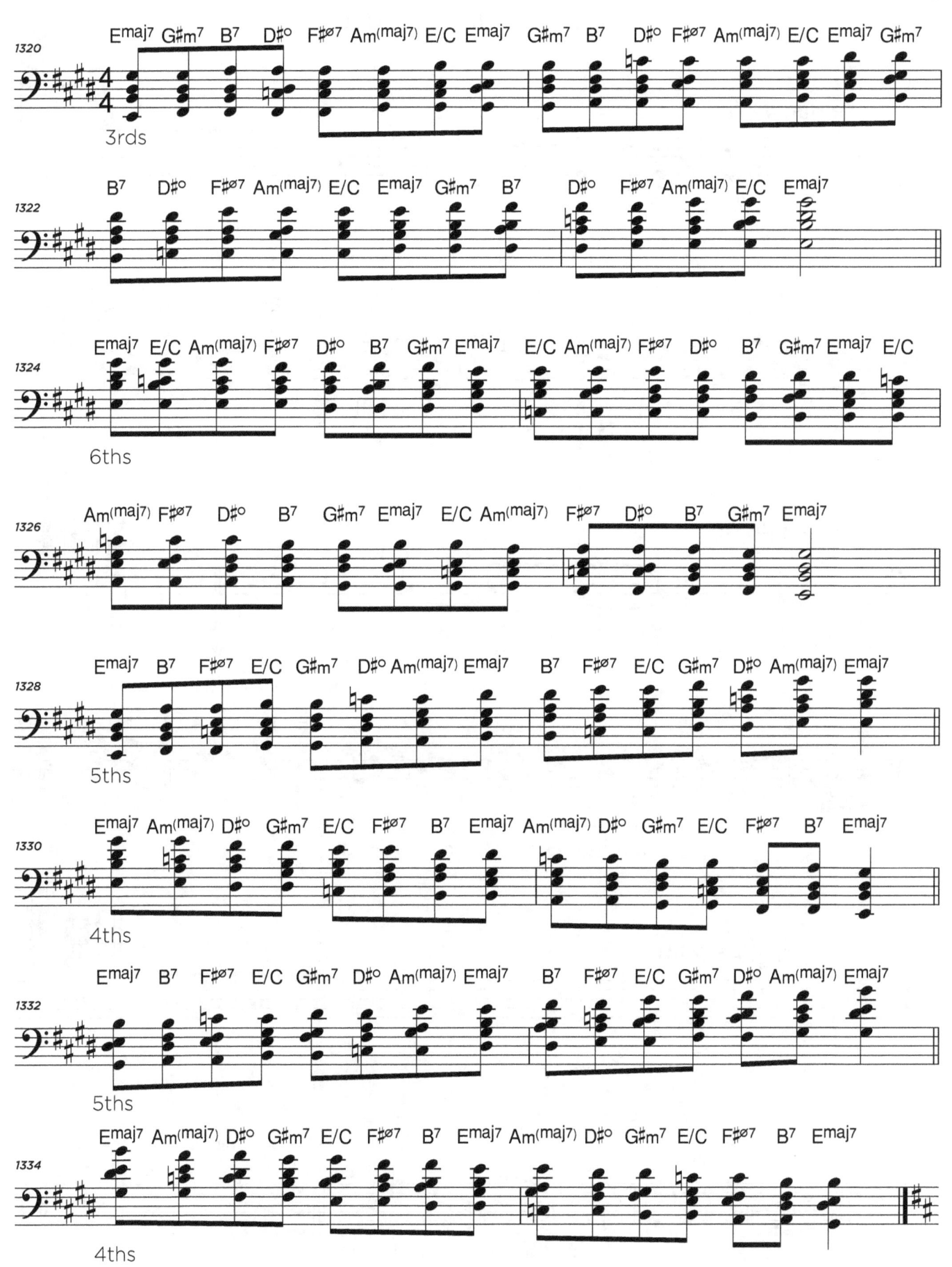

© 2017 by Felix Pastorius

Melodic Minor Modes

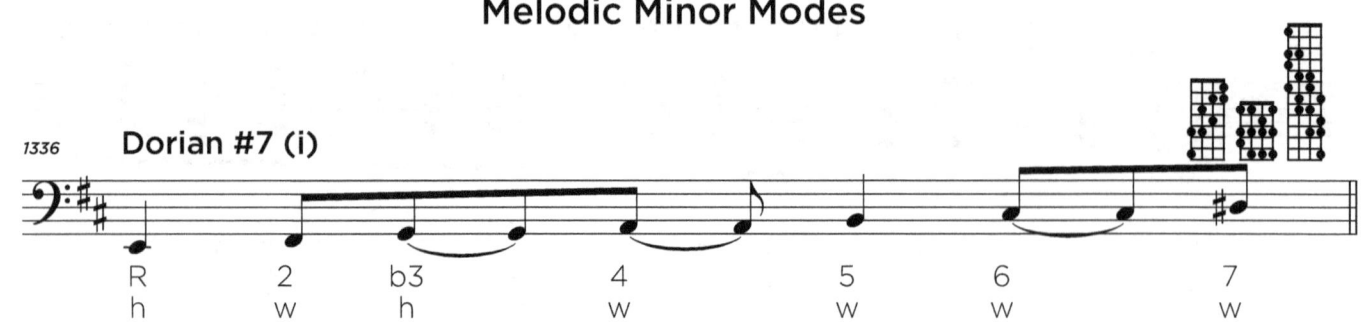

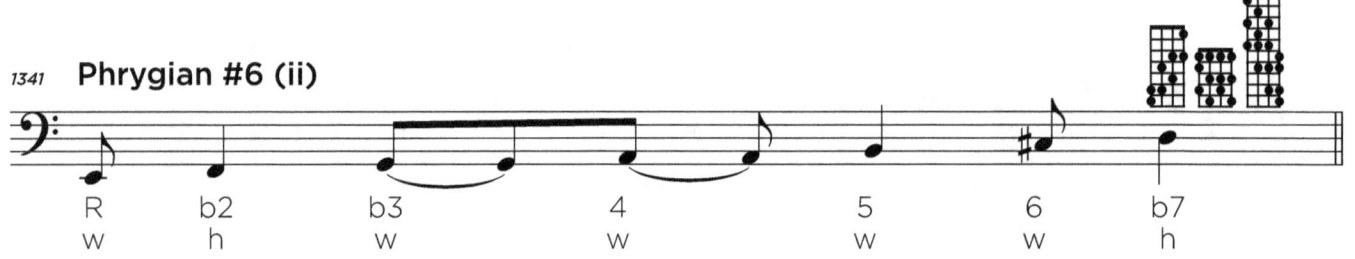

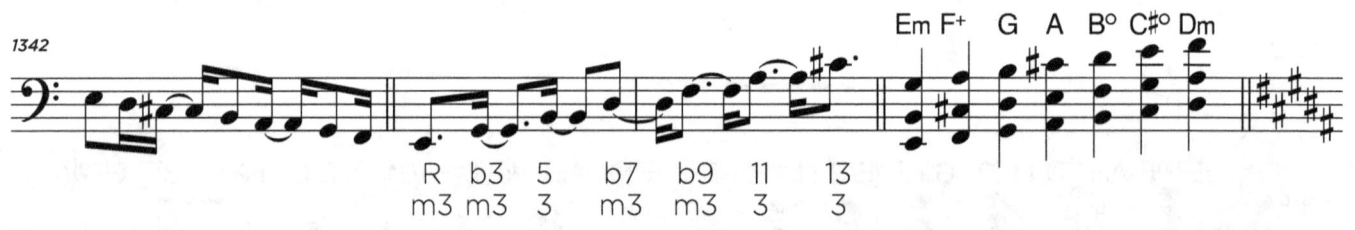

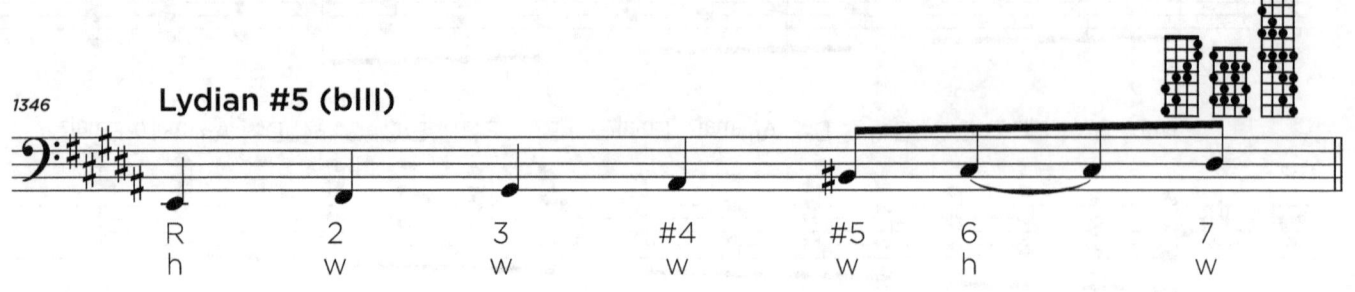

© 2017 by Felix Pastorius

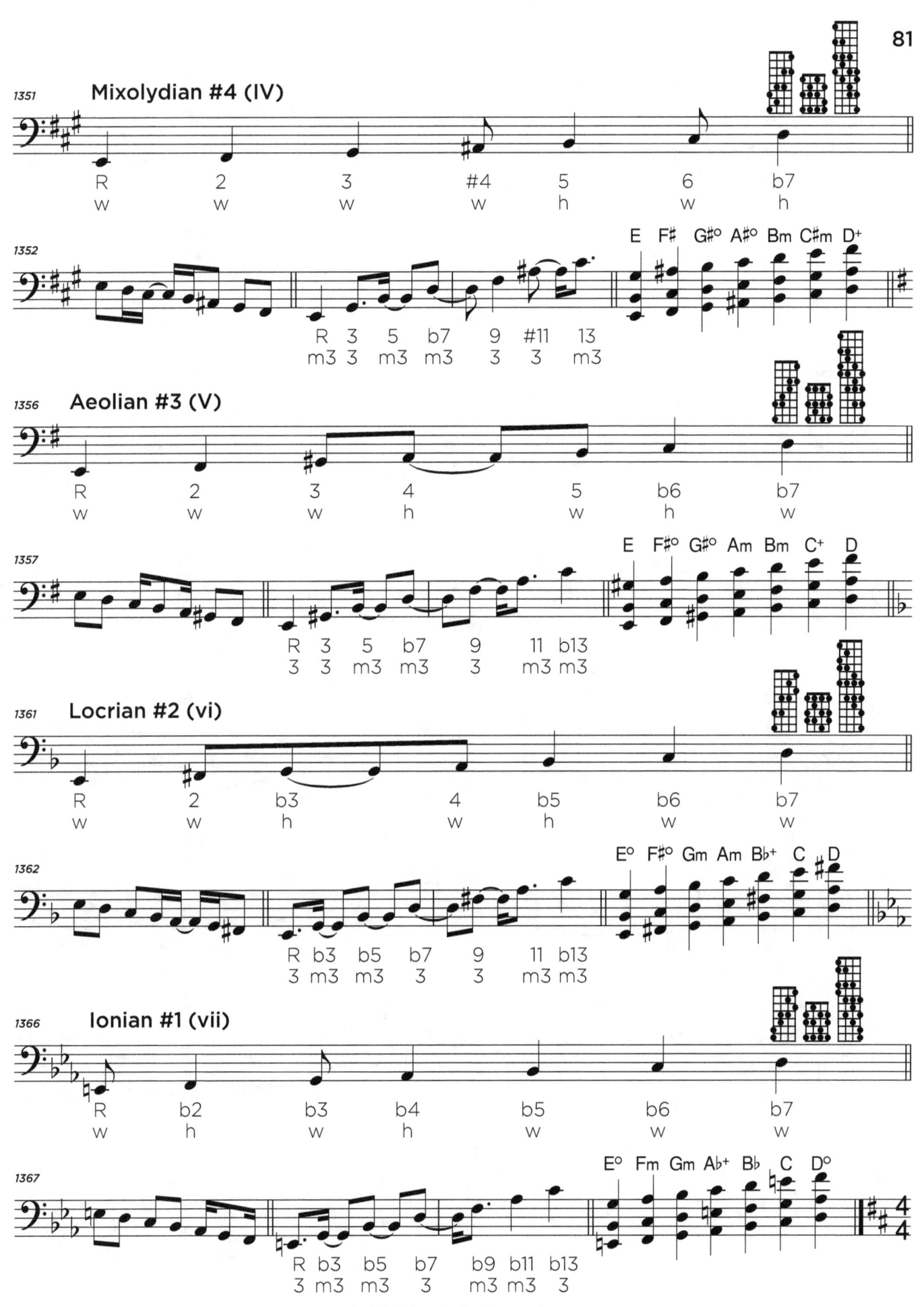

Arpeggios Starting on the Root

Arpeggios Starting on the 3rd

Arpeggios Starting on the 5th

100

© 2017 by Felix Pastorius

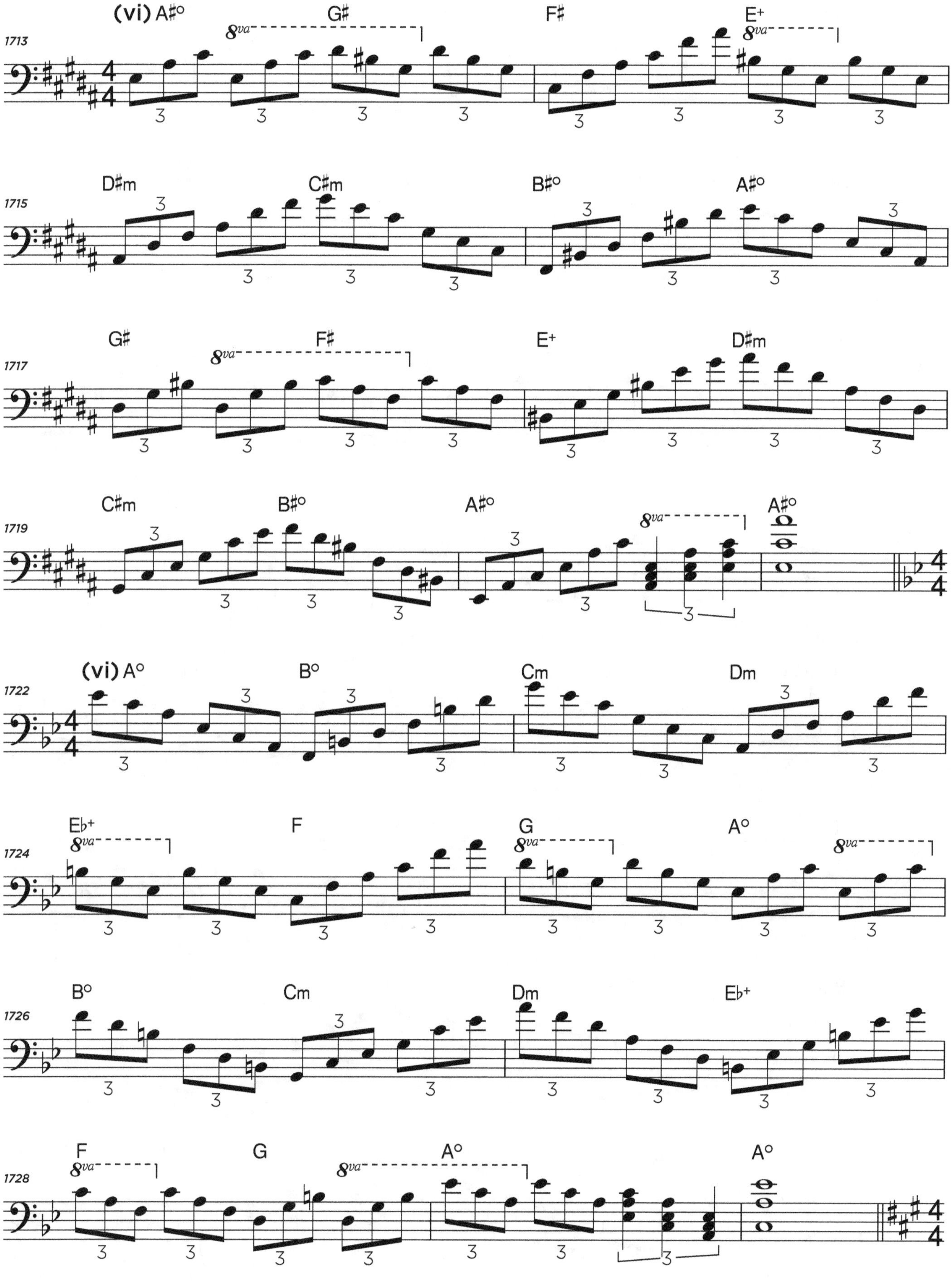
1713 (vi) A♯o G♯ F♯ E+
1715 D♯m C♯m B♯o A♯o
1717 G♯ F♯ E+ D♯m
1719 C♯m B♯o A♯o A♯o
1722 (vi) Ao Bo Cm Dm
1724 E♭+ F G Ao
1726 Bo Cm Dm E♭+
1728 F G Ao Ao

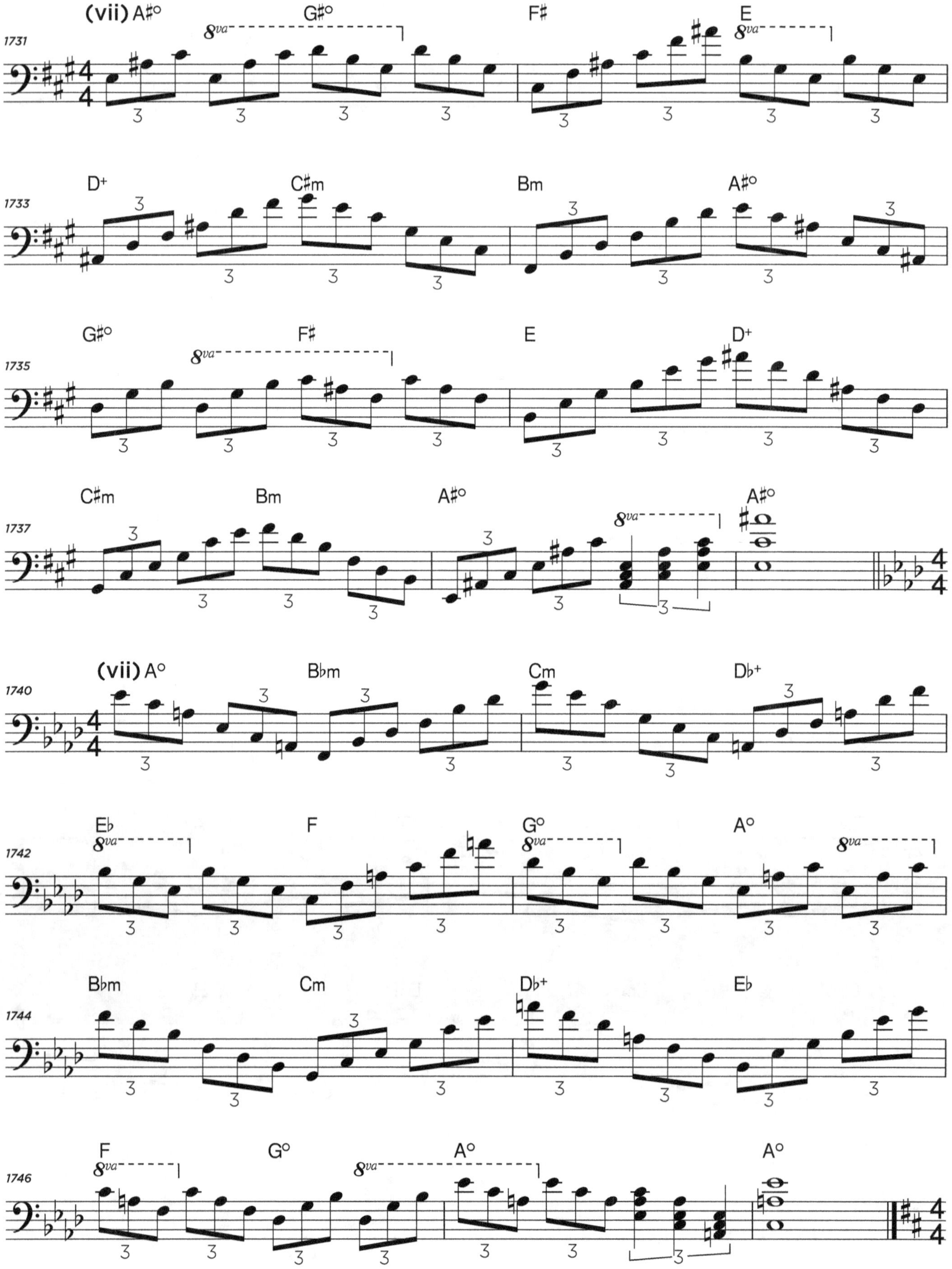
(vii) A♯° G♯° F♯ E
1731
D+ C♯m Bm A♯°
1733
G♯° F♯ E D+
1735
C♯m Bm A♯° A♯°
1737
(vii) A° B♭m Cm D♭+
1740
E♭ F G° A°
1742
B♭m Cm D♭+ E♭
1744
F G° A° A°
1746

Variation #4

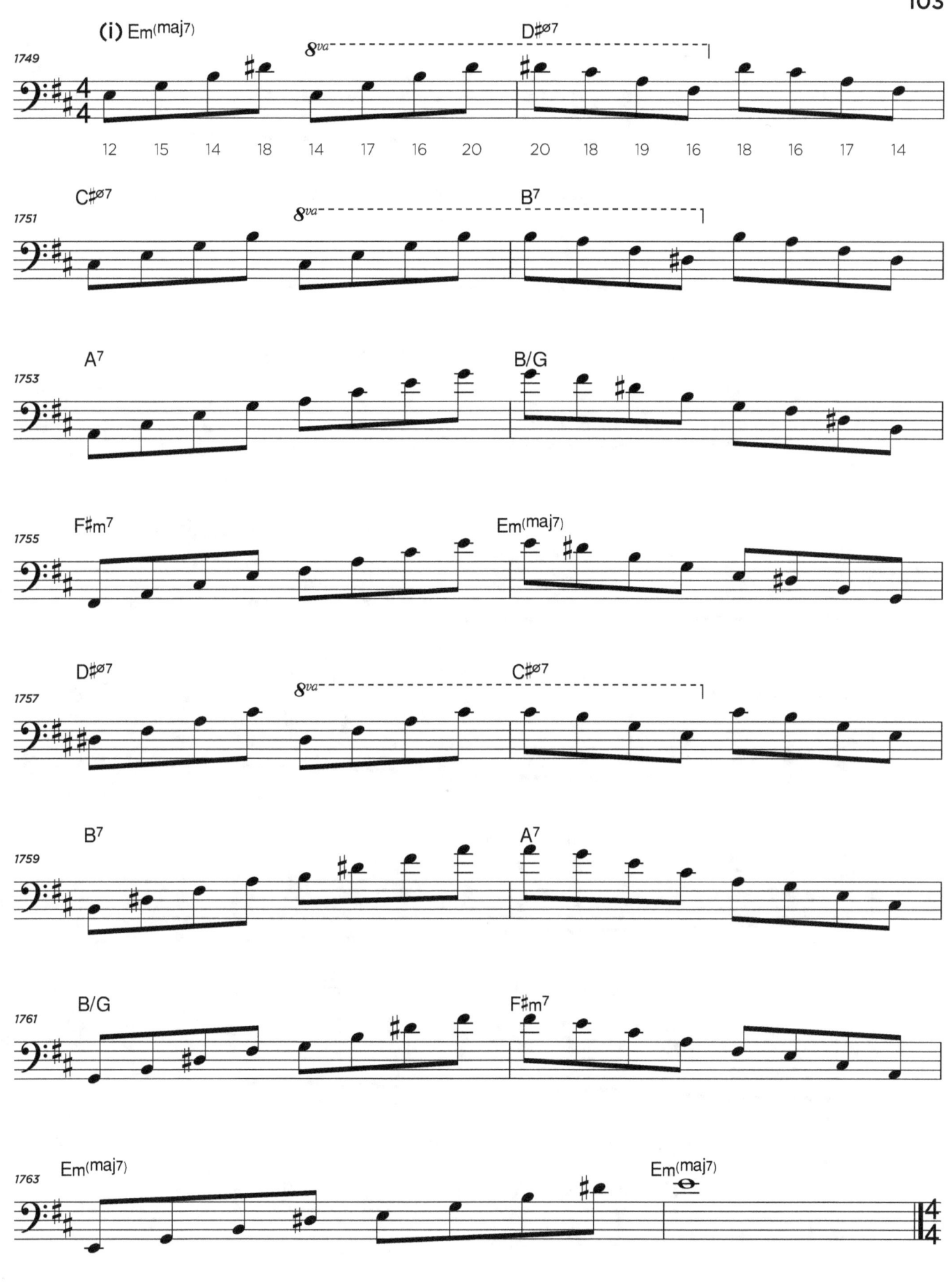

Voice Leading 7th Chords

Breathe

105

1781

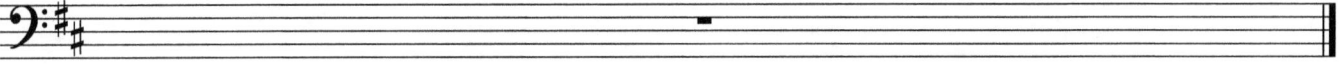

www.ingramcontent.com/pod-product-compliance
Lightning Source LLC
Chambersburg PA
CBHW081420300426
44110CB00016BA/2333